Notes to the Mental Hospital Timekeeper

Notes to the Mental Hospital Timekeeper

Poems by

Tim Mayo

© 2019 Tim Mayo. All rights reserved.
This material may not be reproduced in any form, published,
reprinted, recorded, performed, broadcast,
rewritten or redistributed without
the explicit permission of Tim Mayo.
All such actions are strictly prohibited by law.

Cover design by Shay Culligan

Cover art by Amelia K. Hancock

ISBN: 978-1-950462-56-8

Kelsay Books Inc.

kelsaybooks.com

502 S 1040 E, A119
American Fork, Utah 84003

Acknowledgments

Many thanks to Patricia Fargnoli, whose support and advice were indispensable to this chapbook, and the Vermont Studio Center, where some of these poems were written. Also thanks to the following journals, where these poems were previously published:

The American Journal of Poetry: "The Moral of the Story"
Avatar Review: "The Black Wolf of Your Past," "The Hermit's Tale," and "Victor of Aveyron"
Crosswinds Poetry Journal: "The Ladder" (Honorable Mention for 2019 Crosswinds Poetry Contest)
Connotation Press: An Online Artifact: "Puppet Therapy," which was subsequently published in *Thesaurus of Separation* (Phoenicia Publishing, 2016)
COG Magazine: "Pressure Cooker"
Naugatuck River Review: "Note to the Mental Hospital Timekeeper"
Nine Muses Poetry: "A Brief Explanation of the Psychotic Universe" and "Bagatelle to Stay Awake on Night Shifts"
ONE: "The Elephant in the Room"
Poet Lore: "The Frog and the Snake," which was subsequently published in *The Kingdom of Possibilities* (Mayapple Press, 2009)
Prachya Review: "A Game of Cards" and "Fairy Tale for a Young Inpatient"
San Pedro River Review: "Fugue"
Verse-Virtual: for the reprinting of "The Back Wolf of Your Past" and "The Ladder"
The Worcester Review: "The March Hare"

Contents

A Brief Explanation of the Psychotic Universe	11
A Game of Cards	12
The Black Wolf of Your Past	14
The Elephant in the Room	15
The March Hare	16
Pressure Cooker	21
The Frog and the Snake	22
The Hermit's Tale	24
Victor of Aveyron	29
Fugue	31
Bagatelle to Stay Awake on Night Shifts	34
Fairy Tale for a Young Inpatient	35
Puppet Therapy	39
The Moral of the Story	41
Note to the Mental Hospital Timekeeper	44
The Ladder	46

A Brief Explanation of the Psychotic Universe

This is how it works: the invisible
cause and effect of the universe,
that Big Bang no one has ever heard,
emits its waves of singular commands.

Then the voices ripple through the cosmos,
one by one, whispering their secret orders,
which only I can hear, for I am Cassandra.
I see them slipping into my ear, shifting
with each surreptitious twist of air, skating
the thin line between wind and waft until,
with a flutter, a momentary lull settles
into my head telling me it's time.

Friends, penitents, suffering pilgrims,
all blessed in your hospital blues,
listen, for I have heard the universe,
the first echoes of its birth, nearing
louder and louder with each new gust,
and I alone have escaped to tell you.

A Game of Cards

Night finally came. I had already
turned on the overhead light
illuminating the room,
its different shades of gray,
when my patient suggested
that we play a game of cards.

I thought about this.
I had long ago given up on chance
and was steering my life
toward the certainties I had begun
to learn were truly there.

These were not certainties as one knows facts today
with their tangible logic as hard as rock
and as immutable as the progression of multiplication tables
always moving toward their unavoidable answers.
Those were the mental traps of a mundane mind.

Instead, my certainties were a kind of wisdom,
which emitted from a veiled, capuchin-clad figure
that I noticed followed behind me
wherever I went.

At each moment of indecision on my part,
when I would find myself at a crossroads
where the vanishing point to each choice
showed nothing but a vague promise
diminishing into the distance,

it would whisper to me, imparting
its knowledge into one ear or the other
(it had no true preference)
always telling me the whys and therefores
of the options I was contemplating.

Of course, no one else saw this.
Why should they? The figure
was obviously there only for me.

But to try and explain to you what it was
I should start by saying what it was not.
Although it was loath to speak anything
more than the advice it gave,
it was not a guardian angel.
This much it had confessed to me.

Nonetheless, I began to look upon it
as a higher force from a not so ancient past,
whose physical and spiritual being had been
so deformed by the misfortunes of its own life,

that in its current configuration it had willed itself
to maintain a presence in the nether wake
all mortals make moving through the world
and to advise the mortal it followed
how to thwart the tragedies and mishaps
the figure had already lived.

The overhead light flickered once,
and my patient interrupted my thoughts
insisting we begin our game.

My poor, delusional patient,
whose white garb and guileless expression
belied the true wiles of his mind.

He laid his first card down, telling me
in his earnest, matter of fact manner
how he would beat me, that his sense of numbers
and his memory were better than mine,
so for him, this, too, was no game of chance.

The Black Wolf of Your Past

Suppose you do change your life,
and the black wolf,

which was once your shadow,
silently howls against this extinction.

What do you *then* do for this feral
darkness out of which you grew,

which has trailed you all your life
with a loyalty reserved for pets?

You see it cower, shrink back—deep
into the dog-house of your thoughts,

the long leash of its reach diminished.

What do you do for this wolf
you have fed since birth . . .

throw it a bone?

The Elephant in the Room

Thick skinned, wrinkled and gray,
it sits surrounded by eggshells
you must walk on but not disturb.

Deus of denial and false complacency,
ancient demon of faltering families,
just when you think it's disappeared
like an obsolete religion, fear of god,

out of the corner of your eye, you see
its long reach snake up to sniff you out,
you see it sit again in the easy chair
by the standing lamp, cross its legs,

all big-eared and selectively deaf,
then snap open the paper like a whip,
make you jump—crush the shells.

The March Hare

♪ *Matchmaker, Matchmaker, Make Me a Match* ♪

It was almost the end of the shift,
someone on the Muzak above was playing
a bebop version of *Matchmaker*,
when one of the patients sauntered over.
Slouching in front of me, he hooked his thumbs
into his belt loops, spread his legs apart
and rocked back and forth copping
a kind of wise guy, cowboy attitude.
He said he wanted to leave, and he understood
the best way to *get outta Dodge* was to get
married, and then, he could leave tonight.
I could call him a cab, but first,
I had to find him a woman to marry.

He must have been sizing me up all night.
I'd been hanging out in a nice comfy
armchair, with a modern, cartoonish
pattern of outsized flowers in a soothing,
non-violent color scheme that went well
with the rest of the unit's subtle decor.
The tune, piping down from the ceiling,
changed to something I couldn't recognize,
but I was still feeling pretty good: no woman
in my life, music in my ears, and until then,
a quiet night in the tilting house of the hare.

By now, he was looming over me,
intently waiting for my answer. All
six foot six of him, and by his girth,
a good four hundred and fifty pounds—
maybe more. . . . *Well,* I said, as I stood up
to my full five foot nine and a half inches,
*let me look into this. I've got to enquire
to see who's available. It might take a . . .
moment or two, but I'll get right back,*
and I sauntered out of reach whistling
whatever tune was playing—maybe
Hit the Road, Jack with a fast alto sax
squealing out like a tire or *Fifty Ways
to Leave Your Lover,* something memorable
for one man's desire but not another's.

Pressure Cooker

For years after

I could still see the stain
of its round statement

on the kitchen ceiling,
and in my mind's eye

the yellowed noodles
of chicken soup

are hanging there as well:

a salty broth still dripping
from their ends.

But most of all I remember
my mother's sharp cry

after the slow boil's expansion
and the inarticulate sound

of locked metal surrendering
as the cooker hissed

then un-clammed
in full voice.

Only the lid escapes my memory.
Where did it go?

And that sudden unsealing
of a tightly fastened world . . .

The Frog and the Snake

When I was young I came to a garden pool
and watched a snake swallow a frog.

I have meditated long on this
not wishing to leap to the freedom
of just any conclusion as the frog
must have wanted to do,
                    how I saw death's
turbulence reach out touching many around me:
teachers and a woman who pretended to be
my mother, and then not long after the snake
swallowed its prey, my own mother also died.

What I know now was, when she did, I felt
nothing more than I felt watching that frog
move into the mouth of another world,
the marvelous drama of flesh mouthing flesh
and before that, the frog's immobile wish
to be invisible while the snake flickered about
searching.

            How the frog must have struggled
more than my mother did
when she picked up the pistol by her bed
handling it with that casualness in her loose wrists
that comes from drinking too much, and then . . .
the bang.

      It was all over faster than the frog
who had a good half hour to contemplate
as first one leg disappeared, then the other,
until finally his head, eyes bugging impatiently,
backed down the serpent's mouth into the belly
of its transforming future as if bowing
after a long and well played performance.

What I want to confess, though you cannot see,
is that I blinded myself and wandered about
the kingdom of my possibilities for many years.

The Hermit's Tale

I saw how the world was, how it is:
a savage, finned thing nosed me like a dog,
then shot away, uninterested;

octopi arms surrounded me
like flexing veils; bright fish postured,
and I longed for a refuge.

And so, I withdrew to this place
where, at first, breath was so precious
the heart beat wildly.

Then beside me something calcified.
I grew into it as flesh to bone
even though my ear still heard
an unrequited echo beckon.

Yes, I yearned for something more,
something soft as pulp, a bulbous
red throb beneath it all,

something not armored,
gentle—but the world fluxed,
and water blurred my vision.

Now the sea's floor shifts with the tide.
A push-and-pull nudges me along,
rolling, rocking me,
through the rough and tumble sand,

and sand calluses everything,
though my house protects me
wherever I am.

This is where I live, what I know:
the walls of my home
swirl smaller and faster
to a point I cannot see,

and the heart begins
to beat like a snail.

Victor of Aveyron

Speechless, Wild Child moves
namelessly through the leaves,

loping naked on all fours,
knuckling the earth.

Stand up is for wanting
for reaching—sitting
for having and gnawing.

Trees have their tree-ness
sweet handfuls to pick and mouth
but no mouth sound.

Scratches crisscross the matte
smudge of his face:

the whip and lash of brush
he burrows into each night.

Except
for his little, hairless sex
hanging like beans in a pod
he doesn't yet know
how to pick,

he could be girl . . . be animal . . .

or even vegetable but for the inkling
of words people mouth—sounds
which crowd around him like a net,

and their unachievable gargle
which will haunt him
until he dies.

Fugue

Shift change and I am here,
working the locked ward
for adolescents.

The afternoon sun descends
like a dubious gift,

stretching the shadows
behind the short lives
of everyone in its light.

Kids mill about bawling
like street hawkers selling
the bounce and squeeze
of their stress,

a magma bubbles beneath,
while staff, almost as young,
attempt to solidify

the only eruption the kids may make
down to the courtyard
for basketball and Frisbee.

For a moment, I am still here with them,
appearing as organized as my co-worker,
the skittering back and forth
of her eyes trying to count heads.

For a moment I am still present, there,
amid the slap and shuffle of slippers,
amid the shouts and silence of their banter,
the buried wounds of abuse and abandonment,
the buried hurt of failed placements
in foster home after foster home,

all of them clambering in a relentless
commotion against the past—until
a soft and untouchable front slides in
covering me like a deadening blanket,

and the din its silence hides
diminishes into a thin hum.

*

Voices   flutter away,   a gray,   still   blur   arrives,

even the light,   tilting   through the window,

winks out   like a   failed   bulb,   and   there is

<u>no</u>   <u>one</u>   <u>here</u>   existing in this   mute   moment.

Even the forced   absence   of *their*   pain

has squeezed   out of   every pore   of skin

to transcend   body   and   brain   to this

now-diaphanous place,   this   limbo-veil,

where the sabbatical   from color,   feeling,

and sound,   commends this   shrouded self

to this   blank,   numb,   burial-at-sea,   this

limbic zero   of time,   memory   and place.

Bagatelle to Stay Awake on Night Shifts

The scars on my wrists are not what you think.
On one, a dog bit me as I addressed her mistress.
(A quick zip to the hospital sewed me up like new.)
On the other, a shrill girl, mad at her mother, shrieked
and chewed me like the nipple she'd never known.
I want to say I'm a better person for having been
consumed by fear, anger, and the animal love
of those we want to love and be loved by—*but* . . .

let me just surreptitiously whisper what I've become,
lisp out a little *psst* between these gaps in time and teeth,
when we lick our wounds with words and dreams.
I am the tooth fairy, come to collect the ivory loss
of the unloved, the impressions they make. *Ooh,*
what shall I leave under their pillows tonight?

Fairy Tale for a Young Inpatient

Down, down, way down, at the very bottom
of the old wishing well,
the one with the broken crank, no rope, and no pail,
the one still covered by the quaint,
scant roof meant to keep other things out,

down, down to where the memories you keep
lie at the bottom like tarnished pennies,
one day, there will appear a splendid fish,
as red and as gold as your fabulous cape,
my princess, my forlorn one.

You will see it swim in the deep,
distorting murk we all wish to forget,
fluttering its fins like a fledgling,
testing its way out of the well,
and you will drop a line, a strangling
thread from your cape, unspun in desperation,
trying, once more, to reach beyond
the bottom to where there are no memories.

But, you will catch this fish, instead,
reeling it in like a new story worth telling,
unnoticed until now, though it has always been there
flickering about between the dull coins.

And after you pull up this fish
with its sparkling gossamer fins
you will wrap it gently in the matching
colors of your cape, cradle it in your scarred arms
all the way up the narrow, insufficient pass
of your past with its many twists and turns,

along the whole cruelty of that journey,
then finally down the other side to a calm place,
where the lake water licks the shore in little waves.

There, you will kneel down and surrender
all that you've carried into that clear water,
stretching yourself out to swim with the fish,
the beautiful one you rescued.

Puppet Therapy

I watch a man. Hands toying his totem,
he talks to the group, his fingers
playing out his words on the table.

Everyone leans in a little closer
as he fiddles with a small, green turtle
made of rubber. He explains the sinking
turtle of his self, how he wants to shed
the dark carapace he carries.

*When the day begins to lag, and
the heaviness you're born to sags
through your veins, because the clouds
have muddled the blue right out of your sky,*

*you just drop your soul into the deep mud
of your being. You just stop. Right there.
In the middle of the road. Become a hard lump
against the black tar of the difficult day.*

He shoves the turtle head inside its shell.
This is where he dwells most of his days.

Now he takes a small enameled butterfly
from the table of assorted objects.
It is made of tin. He loves its delicate mobility,

the way it inhabits the air, un-muddied,
not dirigible, the way it doesn't hold the air
inside like a breath you can never expel.

Instead, its wings, replete with color, just twitch, then
flutter, and the whole world leaps happily after.

Somehow, he knows *it is there:*
he feels a bright fluttering in the ribcage
of his gloom that is more than just
the sluggish heart pumping to survive.

He says, *this time,* he will crack the shell;
this time, he will see the quivering inside emerge,
cleave from the hard cocoon of his heaviness,

and he will see its splendid wings spread,
and a gaudy glory will hover all red and yellow
over the green and brown smudge of his life.

The Moral of the Story

So, you've been working detox
for eight years seeing the repeat
business as a curse, grumbling
about how the clients never learn,
not knowing what ever happened
to all those you never see again.
What's wrong with this picture?
The pay's not bad—you're not
the head honcho—but you help people,
and the bennies are better than okay.

Anyway. You run into this guy
on the street. He kind of hops
around with one leg shorter
than the other, and he says
he knows you from work,
but you don't remember him,
and it's pretty clear why
as you listen to the way his whiney voice
seems to be asking for the love
no one ever gave him.

He's smaller than you are
and you're no giant.
But you listen, because that's
what you've learned to do,
and as you look down at him,
he thanks you with downcast eyes
for the many times you did listen
and for the wisdom of those poems
you used to read out loud
before each group you ran.

He tells you he's been sober, now,
for a year—just arrived back in town
and already he's got a night job
at the Sunoco near the interstate.
He jabbers on about how he spent the year
working at the Salvation Army, how he
begins and ends each day with a prayer
and all the minutiae in between,
which have helped his spiritual growth.
He goes on and on until his speech
begins to feel a little forced, a little faster,
and you're not quite following him,
so you fix your eyes on the ground
as if this can help you listen.

Then, . . . he stops . . .

You look up into his eyes; he winces
as he asks if you could help him
get a job like you have.
He wants to *give back a little,
carry the message,* as they say.

You can only imagine what your
wooden, professional face
must look like as you let this sink in,
and you think about how many years
you were sober before you began
this work, but he turns and hops away
before you can answer,

and as you watch him go, suddenly,
you think of Jiminy Cricket.

And then, you think of Pinocchio. . . .
How he changed into a real boy at the end.

Note to the Mental Hospital Timekeeper

Dear Bob,

Today, I subbed at the hospital school,
babysitting class after class,
teaching the kids nothing—the ones
who live across the street
in the group homes the hospital runs.

As you can see from the time clock,
ADP provides both you and me,
it took the allotted six point five hours
before the kids and I gathered up
our coats and hats, calling it a day,
and they trudged back to the locked doors
of their houses, and I climbed the stairs
to the locked door of my garret,
where I write you this poem
instead of my usual email—not about
the extra money I am due—but about
the grains of sand, which seemed
to sift through my fingers, today,
each grain chafing at another life
each child imagines living,
and about the heaviness
weighing on them, drooping
their shoulders like sand bags
the residents of some river town carry
to make the embankments they need
to hold back the imminent flood.

Nonetheless,
please remember to credit me
the higher pay rate I am in fact due,
if only for offering my empty hand,
then for filling it with pencils
I personally sharpened, cursing
the pencil maker for their off-center leads,
as I then gave each student their own wand
to calculate the magic of wisdom
and to mark down the answers
they are trying to find: the true values
of the algebraic x's in the countless
disappointments that make up
the lopsided equations of their lives.

Tomorrow, I'll sub again,
and I promise to send you
another reminder. Until then,
keep the home fires burning
and the old time clock well oiled.
We'll never know—will we?—
when the electric world will fail,
and the spark of connection dies.

The Ladder

Thou shalt love thy neighbor as thyself
                —Matthew 22:37-40

And you see yourself struggling up this ladder
toward some intangible paradigm of self-love,
painfully stepping up from each lower rung
of self-loathing to the next one of lesser loathing,
where you hope to glimpse a kinder, gentler self,
save your soles this soreness of effort,
finally see the beauty in your angular,
asymmetrical face, your awkward gait,
and your slow ability to forgive yourself,
but the balls of your bare feet have become
bruised by each rung's unforgiving resistance
to the weight of your body and purpose,
so you can hardly step up anymore,
when the revelation comes to you
in that sudden balancing act atop the ladder,
now splayed, A-like, to each side of you,
where all the limits of the room: walls, ceiling,
floor, remain out of reach, but nonetheless,
the infinity of love now seems within reach
in that yonder of an ideal world,
as there, in the wobbly stillness, you realize
how walking on air could be the ultimate state,
where the pain of each step would no longer exist,
and the air would embrace you, every part of you,
right down to your black and blue sole, and the air
would embrace everyone—except your neighbor,
the one we haven't yet addressed in this poem,
who stands, grounded, holding your ladder,
tensing every muscle to jump and catch you.

Notes

"The March Hare": "To be as 'mad as a March hare' is an English idiomatic phrase derived from the observed antics, said to occur only in the March breeding season, of the European Hare *Lepus europaeus*. The phrase is an allusion that can be used to refer to any other animal or human who behaves in the excitable and unpredictable manner of a 'March hare.' A long-held view is that the hare will behave strangely and excitedly throughout its breeding season, which in Europe peaks in the month of March. This odd behavior includes boxing at other hares, jumping vertically for seemingly no reason and generally displaying abnormal behavior." (Wikipedia)

"Victor of Aveyron": *l'Enfant sauvage de l'Aveyron,* the story of Victor's discovery during the French Revolution, is often referred to as the first recorded incident of a feral child. It was written by Jean Marc Gaspard Itard, the doctor who took Victor in and tried to "civilize" him and teach him to speak. He finally gave up on Victor, but his monograph about his experience trying to teach Victor is a powerful story, which I read some years ago.

"Fairy Tale for a Young Inpatient": The two things that the nursing staff have to watch out for on the adolescent inpatient unit, where I sometimes work, are attempts by patients to hang or strangle themselves and to make sure that a patient doesn't find any sharp objects to self-harm with usually by cutting their arms. The act of cutting releases dopamine in the brain, which besides acting as a physical pain reliever also acts more importantly as an emotional/psychological pain reliever.

"Note to the Mental Hospital Timekeeper": Automatic Data Processing, Inc., commonly known by its New York Stock Exchange symbol, *ADP,* is a provider of human resources management software and services. There is an online login portal where workers and timekeepers at my hospital can verify the time clock swipes and also where the timekeeper can make notations about pay rates and adjust the time swiped in if one happened to make a mistake swiping in (or forgot). Although most people don't, I happen to work different jobs at different pay rates. Thus, when I clock in, I often need to email the timekeeper to tell him which job I am working so he will credit me the pay rate which applies to that particular job. In a note to this note, this process has since changed, but what I mention above is still relevant to the poem.

About the Author

Tim Mayo holds an ALB, *Cum Laude,* from Harvard University and an MFA from The Bennington Writing Seminars. Among the many places his poems and reviews have appeared are *The American Journal of Poetry, Avatar Review, Barrow Street, Narrative Magazine, Poetry International, Poet Lore, River Styx, Salamander, San Pedro River Review, Tar River Poetry, Valparaiso Poetry Review, Verse Daily, Web Del Sol Review of Books,* and *The Writer's Almanac.* His poems have received seven Pushcart Prize nominations and have twice been finalists for the Paumanok Poetry Award.

His first full length collection, *The Kingdom of Possibilities,* (Mayapple Press, 2009) was a finalist for the 2009 May Swenson Award. His second volume of poems, *Thesaurus of Separation* (Phoenicia Publishing 2016) was a finalist for the 2017 Montaigne Medal and a finalist for the 2017 Eric Hoffer Book Award. He was a founding member of the Brattleboro Literary Festival and is a Substitute Teacher and *per diem* Mental Health Worker at the Brattleboro Retreat.

www.ingramcontent.com/pod-product-compliance
Lightning Source LLC
Chambersburg PA
CBHW021028090426
42738CB00007B/939